50 Gourmet Comfort Sandwich Recipes for Home

By: Kelly Johnson

Table of Contents

- Truffle Mushroom Grilled Cheese
- Buffalo Chicken Melt with Blue Cheese
- Bacon, Egg, and Avocado Toast
- Lobster Roll with Herb Mayonnaise
- Pork Belly Banh Mi
- Caprese Sandwich with Balsamic Glaze
- Smoked Salmon and Cream Cheese Bagel
- Short Rib French Dip with Horseradish Sauce
- Roast Beef and Caramelized Onion Panini
- Pulled Pork with Apple Slaw
- Chicken Parmesan Sub
- Philly Cheesesteak with Sautéed Peppers and Onions
- Grilled Veggie and Hummus Wrap
- Gourmet Monte Cristo with Berry Jam
- Reuben Sandwich with Homemade Sauerkraut
- Cuban Sandwich with Pickles and Mustard
- Fried Chicken and Pickle Sandwich
- Mushroom and Swiss Stuffed Burger
- Braised Lamb and Mint Yogurt Flatbread
- Eggplant Parmesan Sandwich
- Salami and Provolone Ciabatta
- Chicken and Pesto Panini
- Turkey, Cranberry, and Brie Sandwich
- Cheddar and Apple Butter Grilled Cheese
- Beef and Blue Cheese Stuffed Pretzel Roll
- Sweet and Spicy Sausage Sub
- Grilled Chicken Caesar Wrap
- Pulled Pork and Pineapple Slaw Sandwich
- Crispy Tofu Banh Mi
- Tuna Melt with Capers and Pickles
- BBQ Chicken and Cheddar Sandwich
- Avocado and Tomato Basil Sandwich

- Beef Stroganoff Sandwich with Mushrooms
- Crispy Fish Sandwich with Remoulade Sauce
- Turkey Club with Avocado and Bacon
- Braised Beef Brisket with Horseradish Cream
- Buffalo Cauliflower Wrap
- Spicy Italian Sub with Giardiniera
- Grilled Chicken and Mango Chutney Sandwich
- Cheesy Ham and Swiss Croissant
- Pulled Pork and Chipotle BBQ Sandwich
- Pastrami on Rye with Mustard
- Classic Lobster Grilled Cheese
- Spicy Tuna and Avocado Sandwich
- Balsamic Glazed Chicken Sandwich
- Brisket and Pickled Onion Sandwich
- Stuffed Portobello Mushroom Burger
- Pork Schnitzel Sandwich with Cabbage Slaw
- Crispy Chicken Sandwich with Garlic Aioli
- Hot Turkey Sandwich with Gravy

Truffle Mushroom Grilled Cheese

Ingredients:

- 4 slices of sourdough bread
- 2 tablespoons unsalted butter, softened
- 1 cup grated Gruyère cheese
- 1 cup grated fontina cheese
- 1 cup mushrooms, finely chopped (such as cremini or shiitake)
- 2 tablespoons truffle oil
- 1 garlic clove, minced
- 1 tablespoon fresh thyme leaves (or 1 teaspoon dried thyme)
- Salt and pepper to taste
- Optional: 1 tablespoon truffle shavings for garnish

Instructions:

1. **Prepare the Mushrooms:**
    - In a skillet over medium heat, add 1 tablespoon of butter.
    - Once melted, add the chopped mushrooms and cook until they release their moisture and become golden brown, about 5-7 minutes.
    - Add the minced garlic and thyme, and cook for another 1-2 minutes until fragrant.
    - Drizzle the truffle oil over the mushrooms, and season with salt and pepper. Stir to combine.
    - Remove from heat and set aside.
2. **Assemble the Sandwiches:**
    - Spread a thin layer of softened butter on one side of each slice of sourdough bread.
    - On the non-buttered side of two slices, layer the Gruyère and fontina cheeses.
    - Spoon the mushroom mixture evenly over the cheese.
    - Top with the remaining slices of bread, buttered side up.
3. **Grill the Sandwiches:**
    - Heat a skillet over medium heat.
    - Place the sandwiches in the skillet and cook until golden brown and the cheese is melted, about 3-4 minutes per side.
    - Press down slightly with a spatula to ensure even grilling and melty cheese.
4. **Serve:**
    - Remove from the skillet and let rest for a minute.
    - Optionally, garnish with truffle shavings for an extra touch of luxury.
    - Slice and serve warm.

Enjoy your indulgent Truffle Mushroom Grilled Cheese!

Buffalo Chicken Melt with Blue Cheese

Ingredients:

- 2 cups cooked chicken, shredded (such as rotisserie or grilled)
- 1/2 cup buffalo sauce
- 1/4 cup ranch or blue cheese dressing
- 4 slices of sourdough or ciabatta bread
- 1 tablespoon unsalted butter, softened
- 1 cup shredded mozzarella cheese
- 1/2 cup crumbled blue cheese
- Optional: sliced celery for crunch

Instructions:

1. **Prepare the Chicken:**
   - In a bowl, toss the shredded chicken with buffalo sauce until well coated.
2. **Assemble the Sandwiches:**
   - Spread butter on one side of each slice of bread.
   - On the non-buttered side of two slices, spread a layer of ranch or blue cheese dressing.
   - Top with the buffalo chicken mixture.
   - Sprinkle mozzarella and crumbled blue cheese on top of the chicken.
   - Place the remaining slices of bread on top, buttered side up.
3. **Grill the Sandwiches:**
   - Heat a skillet over medium heat.
   - Place the sandwiches in the skillet and cook until golden brown and the cheese is melted, about 3-4 minutes per side.
   - Press down slightly with a spatula to ensure even grilling and melting.
4. **Serve:**
   - Remove from the skillet and let rest for a minute.
   - Optionally, garnish with sliced celery for added crunch.
   - Slice and serve warm.

Enjoy your spicy and cheesy Buffalo Chicken Melt!

Bacon, Egg, and Avocado Toast

Ingredients:

- 4 slices of sourdough or whole-grain bread
- 4 slices of bacon
- 2 ripe avocados
- 1 tablespoon lemon juice (optional, to prevent browning)
- Salt and pepper to taste
- 4 large eggs
- 2 tablespoons unsalted butter or olive oil
- Red pepper flakes or hot sauce (optional, for added flavor)
- Chopped fresh chives or parsley (optional, for garnish)

Instructions:

1. **Cook the Bacon:**
    - Heat a skillet over medium heat.
    - Add the bacon slices and cook until crispy, about 5-7 minutes, turning occasionally.
    - Transfer the cooked bacon to a paper towel-lined plate to drain excess fat.
2. **Prepare the Avocado:**
    - Cut the avocados in half, remove the pits, and scoop the flesh into a bowl.
    - Mash the avocado with a fork. If desired, mix in lemon juice to keep the avocado from browning.
    - Season with salt and pepper to taste.
3. **Cook the Eggs:**
    - In the same skillet used for the bacon (or a separate skillet), heat 2 tablespoons of butter or olive oil over medium-low heat.
    - Crack the eggs into the skillet and cook until the whites are set and the yolks are cooked to your preference (sunny-side up or over-easy).
    - Season with salt and pepper.
4. **Toast the Bread:**
    - Toast the bread slices in a toaster or on a grill pan until golden and crispy.
5. **Assemble the Toast:**
    - Spread a generous layer of mashed avocado on each slice of toasted bread.
    - Top with two slices of bacon per toast.
    - Carefully place a cooked egg on top of the bacon.
    - Sprinkle with red pepper flakes or drizzle with hot sauce if desired.
    - Garnish with chopped chives or parsley for added freshness.
6. **Serve:**
    - Serve immediately while the toast is still warm and the egg is still runny.

Enjoy your hearty and flavorful Bacon, Egg, and Avocado Toast!

Lobster Roll with Herb Mayonnaise

Ingredients:

For the Lobster Filling:

- 1 pound cooked lobster meat, chopped (about 2 lobster tails)
- 2 tablespoons unsalted butter
- 1 tablespoon lemon juice
- 1 tablespoon fresh chives, chopped
- 1 tablespoon fresh parsley, chopped
- 1 tablespoon fresh tarragon, chopped (optional)
- Salt and pepper to taste

For the Herb Mayonnaise:

- 1/2 cup mayonnaise
- 1 tablespoon fresh chives, finely chopped
- 1 tablespoon fresh parsley, finely chopped
- 1 teaspoon fresh lemon juice
- 1 teaspoon Dijon mustard
- Salt and pepper to taste

For Assembly:

- 4 New England-style hot dog buns or split-top rolls
- 1 tablespoon unsalted butter, melted
- Lemon wedges for serving (optional)

Instructions:

1. **Prepare the Herb Mayonnaise:**
    - In a small bowl, mix together the mayonnaise, chives, parsley, lemon juice, Dijon mustard, salt, and pepper.
    - Adjust seasoning to taste and set aside.
2. **Prepare the Lobster Filling:**
    - In a skillet over medium heat, melt the butter.
    - Add the chopped lobster meat and cook until heated through, about 2-3 minutes.
    - Stir in the lemon juice, chives, parsley, tarragon (if using), salt, and pepper.
    - Remove from heat and set aside.
3. **Prepare the Buns:**
    - Preheat a skillet or griddle over medium heat.
    - Brush the outside of each bun with melted butter.
    - Toast the buns in the skillet until golden brown and crisp, about 2 minutes per side.

4. **Assemble the Lobster Rolls:**
    - Spread a generous amount of the herb mayonnaise on the inside of each toasted bun.
    - Fill each bun with the warm lobster mixture.
5. **Serve:**
    - Serve the lobster rolls immediately with lemon wedges on the side, if desired.

Enjoy your luxurious and flavorful Lobster Roll with Herb Mayonnaise!

Pork Belly Banh Mi

Ingredients:

For the Pork Belly:

- 1 pound pork belly, skin removed
- 1 tablespoon soy sauce
- 1 tablespoon hoisin sauce
- 1 tablespoon fish sauce
- 1 tablespoon brown sugar
- 2 cloves garlic, minced
- 1 tablespoon grated ginger
- 1/2 teaspoon five-spice powder
- 1/4 teaspoon black pepper

For the Pickled Vegetables:

- 1 cup carrots, julienned
- 1 cup daikon radish, julienned
- 1/2 cup rice vinegar
- 1/2 cup water
- 1/4 cup sugar
- 1/4 teaspoon salt

For Assembly:

- 4 French baguettes or Vietnamese baguettes
- 1/2 cup mayonnaise
- 1 tablespoon sriracha or hot sauce (optional)
- 1/2 cup cilantro leaves
- 1 jalapeño, thinly sliced (optional)
- Cucumber slices for crunch (optional)

Instructions:

1. **Prepare the Pork Belly:**
    - Preheat your oven to 300°F (150°C).
    - In a small bowl, mix together the soy sauce, hoisin sauce, fish sauce, brown sugar, garlic, ginger, five-spice powder, and black pepper.
    - Rub the pork belly with the mixture and place it on a rack set inside a baking dish.
    - Roast the pork belly in the preheated oven for 2 to 2.5 hours, or until tender. (Alternatively, you can cook it in a slow cooker on low for 6-8 hours.)
    - Remove from the oven and let it rest for 15 minutes. Slice into thin strips.

2. **Prepare the Pickled Vegetables:**
   - In a bowl, combine the rice vinegar, water, sugar, and salt. Stir until the sugar and salt are dissolved.
   - Add the julienned carrots and daikon radish to the mixture. Let them pickle for at least 30 minutes (or up to several hours in the refrigerator).
3. **Prepare the Baguettes:**
   - Slice the baguettes lengthwise, leaving one side attached to create a pocket.
4. **Assemble the Banh Mi:**
   - Mix the mayonnaise with sriracha or hot sauce if using.
   - Spread a layer of mayonnaise on the inside of each baguette.
   - Layer the sliced pork belly inside the baguette.
   - Top with pickled vegetables, cilantro leaves, and optional jalapeño slices and cucumber slices.
5. **Serve:**
   - Serve immediately while the baguettes are still crisp.

Enjoy your flavorful and authentic Pork Belly Banh Mi!

Caprese Sandwich with Balsamic Glaze

Ingredients:

- 4 slices of ciabatta or Italian bread
- 1 tablespoon olive oil
- 1 cup fresh mozzarella, sliced
- 1 large tomato, sliced
- Fresh basil leaves
- Salt and pepper to taste

For the Balsamic Glaze:

- 1/2 cup balsamic vinegar
- 2 tablespoons honey or brown sugar

Instructions:

1. **Prepare the Balsamic Glaze:**
   - In a small saucepan, combine the balsamic vinegar and honey (or brown sugar).
   - Bring to a simmer over medium heat, stirring frequently.
   - Cook until the mixture reduces by half and thickens to a syrupy consistency, about 10 minutes.
   - Remove from heat and let cool.
2. **Prepare the Sandwiches:**
   - Preheat a grill pan or skillet over medium heat.
   - Brush the slices of bread with olive oil on one side.
   - Place the bread, oiled side down, in the pan and toast until golden brown, about 2-3 minutes per side.
3. **Assemble the Sandwiches:**
   - On the toasted side of two slices of bread, layer slices of fresh mozzarella and tomato.
   - Season with salt and pepper.
   - Top with fresh basil leaves.
   - Drizzle with balsamic glaze.
   - Place the remaining slices of toasted bread on top to form a sandwich.
4. **Serve:**
   - Cut the sandwiches in half and serve immediately.

Enjoy your refreshing Caprese Sandwich with Balsamic Glaze!

Smoked Salmon and Cream Cheese Bagel

Ingredients:

- 2 plain or everything bagels
- 4 ounces cream cheese, softened
- 4 ounces smoked salmon, sliced
- 1/2 small red onion, thinly sliced
- Capers (optional)
- Fresh dill or chives, chopped (optional)
- Lemon wedges (optional)
- Salt and pepper to taste

Instructions:

1. **Prepare the Bagels:**
    - Slice the bagels in half.
    - Toast the bagels to your preferred level of crispness, either in a toaster or under a broiler.
2. **Spread the Cream Cheese:**
    - Evenly spread the softened cream cheese over the cut sides of each toasted bagel.
3. **Add the Smoked Salmon:**
    - Layer the smoked salmon slices over the cream cheese on each bagel half.
4. **Add Toppings:**
    - Top with thin slices of red onion.
    - Add capers if using, and sprinkle with freshly chopped dill or chives if desired.
    - Season with a little salt and freshly ground black pepper.
5. **Serve:**
    - Serve immediately with lemon wedges on the side if desired.

Enjoy your delicious Smoked Salmon and Cream Cheese Bagel!

Short Rib French Dip with Horseradish Sauce

Ingredients:

For the Short Ribs:

- 2 pounds beef short ribs
- 1 tablespoon olive oil
- 1 onion, chopped
- 2 cloves garlic, minced
- 1 cup beef broth
- 1/2 cup red wine (optional)
- 2 tablespoons soy sauce
- 1 tablespoon Worcestershire sauce
- 1 teaspoon dried thyme
- Salt and pepper to taste

For the Horseradish Sauce:

- 1/2 cup sour cream
- 2 tablespoons prepared horseradish
- 1 tablespoon Dijon mustard
- 1 tablespoon lemon juice
- Salt and pepper to taste

For Assembly:

- 4 French rolls or hoagie buns
- 1 cup Swiss cheese or provolone, sliced

Instructions:

1. **Cook the Short Ribs:**
   - Preheat your oven to 300°F (150°C).
   - Heat olive oil in a large ovenproof pot over medium-high heat.
   - Season short ribs with salt and pepper, then sear on all sides until browned. Remove and set aside.
   - In the same pot, add onion and garlic; cook until softened.
   - Return the short ribs to the pot, and add beef broth, red wine (if using), soy sauce, Worcestershire sauce, and thyme.
   - Cover and transfer to the oven. Cook for 2.5 to 3 hours, or until the meat is tender and easily shreds.
2. **Prepare the Horseradish Sauce:**
   - In a small bowl, mix together sour cream, horseradish, Dijon mustard, lemon juice, salt, and pepper. Adjust seasoning to taste.

3. **Shred the Meat:**
    - Remove the short ribs from the pot and shred the meat using two forks. Discard any bones and excess fat.
    - Return the shredded meat to the pot with the cooking juices.
4. **Prepare the Rolls:**
    - Preheat a broiler or grill pan.
    - Slice the French rolls or hoagie buns and place them cut side up on a baking sheet.
    - Top with sliced cheese and broil until melted and bubbly, about 1-2 minutes.
5. **Assemble the Sandwiches:**
    - Divide the shredded short rib mixture among the toasted rolls.
    - Serve with the horseradish sauce on the side for dipping.

Enjoy your flavorful Short Rib French Dip with Horseradish Sauce!

Roast Beef and Caramelized Onion Panini

Ingredients:

- 4 ciabatta rolls or slices of rustic bread
- 2 tablespoons olive oil
- 1 large onion, thinly sliced
- 1 teaspoon brown sugar
- 1 pound roast beef, thinly sliced
- 4 ounces provolone or Swiss cheese, sliced
- 2 tablespoons Dijon mustard
- Salt and pepper to taste

Instructions:

1. **Caramelize the Onions:**
    - Heat olive oil in a skillet over medium heat.
    - Add sliced onions and cook, stirring occasionally, until softened and golden brown, about 15-20 minutes.
    - Stir in brown sugar and season with salt and pepper. Cook for another 2 minutes. Remove from heat.
2. **Assemble the Panini:**
    - Preheat a panini press or skillet over medium heat.
    - Spread Dijon mustard on the inside of each bread slice or roll.
    - Layer with roast beef, caramelized onions, and cheese.
3. **Grill the Panini:**
    - Brush the outside of each sandwich with olive oil.
    - Place sandwiches in the panini press or skillet. If using a skillet, press down with another heavy pan.
    - Grill until the bread is golden brown and the cheese is melted, about 3-4 minutes per side.
4. **Serve:**
    - Cut the panini in half and serve warm.

Enjoy your delicious Roast Beef and Caramelized Onion Panini!

Pulled Pork with Apple Slaw

Ingredients:

For the Pulled Pork:

- 2 pounds pork shoulder (or butt)
- 1 tablespoon olive oil
- 1 onion, chopped
- 3 cloves garlic, minced
- 1 cup BBQ sauce (your favorite)
- 1/2 cup chicken broth
- 1 tablespoon apple cider vinegar
- 1 tablespoon brown sugar
- 1 teaspoon smoked paprika
- Salt and pepper to taste

For the Apple Slaw:

- 2 cups shredded cabbage
- 1 large apple, julienned or thinly sliced
- 1/4 cup mayonnaise
- 1 tablespoon apple cider vinegar
- 1 tablespoon honey
- 1 teaspoon Dijon mustard
- Salt and pepper to taste

For Assembly:

- **4 hamburger buns or slider rolls**

Instructions:

1. **Cook the Pulled Pork:**
    - Preheat your oven to 300°F (150°C).
    - In a large ovenproof pot or Dutch oven, heat olive oil over medium-high heat.
    - Season the pork with salt and pepper, then sear on all sides until browned.
    - Remove the pork and set aside. In the same pot, add onion and garlic; cook until softened.
    - Return the pork to the pot and add BBQ sauce, chicken broth, apple cider vinegar, brown sugar, and smoked paprika.
    - Cover and transfer to the oven. Cook for 3-4 hours, or until the pork is tender and shreds easily with a fork.
    - Remove the pork from the pot, shred it, and return to the pot to mix with the sauce.

2. **Prepare the Apple Slaw:**
    - In a large bowl, combine shredded cabbage and julienned apple.
    - In a small bowl, whisk together mayonnaise, apple cider vinegar, honey, Dijon mustard, salt, and pepper.
    - Toss the cabbage and apple with the dressing until well coated.
3. **Assemble the Sandwiches:**
    - Toast the buns if desired.
    - Pile the pulled pork onto the bottom half of each bun.
    - Top with a generous amount of apple slaw.
    - Place the top half of the bun on each sandwich.
4. **Serve:**
    - Serve the sandwiches warm.

Enjoy your flavorful Pulled Pork with Apple Slaw!

Chicken Parmesan Sub

Ingredients:

- 4 sub rolls or hoagie buns
- 2 cups marinara sauce
- 1 cup all-purpose flour
- 2 large eggs, beaten
- 2 cups breadcrumbs (Italian or plain)
- 1 cup grated Parmesan cheese
- 2 cups shredded mozzarella cheese
- 4 boneless, skinless chicken breasts
- 1/2 cup vegetable oil (for frying)
- Salt and pepper to taste
- Fresh basil or parsley for garnish (optional)

Instructions:

1. **Prepare the Chicken:**
    - Preheat your oven to 375°F (190°C).
    - Pound the chicken breasts to an even thickness between two pieces of plastic wrap.
    - Season the chicken with salt and pepper.
    - Dredge each piece of chicken in flour, then dip in beaten eggs, and coat with breadcrumbs mixed with Parmesan cheese.
2. **Fry the Chicken:**
    - Heat vegetable oil in a large skillet over medium heat.
    - Fry the chicken until golden brown and cooked through, about 4-5 minutes per side.
    - Transfer the chicken to a paper towel-lined plate to drain.
3. **Assemble the Subs:**
    - Slice the sub rolls and lightly toast them if desired.
    - Place a fried chicken breast on each roll.
    - Spoon marinara sauce over the chicken.
    - Top with shredded mozzarella cheese.
4. **Bake the Subs:**
    - Place the assembled subs on a baking sheet.
    - Bake in the preheated oven until the cheese is melted and bubbly, about 10 minutes.
5. **Serve:**
    - Garnish with fresh basil or parsley if desired.
    - Serve warm.

Enjoy your delicious Chicken Parmesan Sub!

Philly Cheesesteak with Sautéed Peppers and Onions

Ingredients:

For the Philly Cheesesteak:

- 1 pound ribeye steak or sirloin, thinly sliced (freeze the steak for 30 minutes to make slicing easier)
- 1 tablespoon olive oil
- Salt and pepper to taste
- 4 hoagie rolls or sub rolls

For the Sautéed Peppers and Onions:

- 1 tablespoon olive oil
- 1 large onion, thinly sliced
- 1 bell pepper, thinly sliced (any color)
- 1 bell pepper, thinly sliced (another color for variety)
- Salt and pepper to taste

For Assembly:

- 4 slices provolone cheese (or American cheese)
- Optional: 1 tablespoon mayonnaise or mustard (for spreading on the rolls)

Instructions:

1. **Prepare the Peppers and Onions:**
   - Heat olive oil in a large skillet over medium heat.
   - Add the sliced onions and bell peppers. Cook, stirring occasionally, until the vegetables are softened and caramelized, about 10-12 minutes.
   - Season with salt and pepper to taste. Set aside.
2. **Cook the Steak:**
   - In a large skillet or griddle over medium-high heat, heat olive oil.
   - Add the thinly sliced steak in a single layer. Cook until browned and cooked through, about 2-3 minutes per side. If cooking in batches, transfer cooked steak to a plate and keep warm.
   - Season with salt and pepper.
3. **Assemble the Cheesesteaks:**
   - Preheat the oven broiler.
   - Slice the hoagie rolls lengthwise, but not all the way through, leaving one side attached.
   - Optional: Spread mayonnaise or mustard on the inside of the rolls.
   - Divide the cooked steak evenly among the rolls.
   - Top each with sautéed peppers and onions.

       - Place a slice of provolone cheese on top of each sandwich.
4. **Broil the Sandwiches:**
       - Place the sandwiches under the broiler for 1-2 minutes, or until the cheese is melted and bubbly. Keep an eye on them to avoid burning.
5. **Serve:**
       - Remove from the oven and serve immediately.

Enjoy your classic Philly Cheesesteak with Sautéed Peppers and Onions!

Grilled Veggie and Hummus Wrap

Ingredients:

- 4 large whole wheat or spinach tortillas
- 1 zucchini, sliced
- 1 red bell pepper, sliced
- 1 yellow bell pepper, sliced
- 1 small red onion, sliced
- 1 tablespoon olive oil
- Salt and pepper to taste
- 1 cup hummus (store-bought or homemade)
- 1 cup baby spinach or mixed greens
- 1/2 cup crumbled feta cheese (optional)
- 1/4 cup kalamata olives, sliced (optional)

Instructions:

1. **Grill the Vegetables:**
    - Preheat a grill or grill pan to medium-high heat.
    - Toss the sliced zucchini, red bell pepper, yellow bell pepper, and red onion with olive oil, salt, and pepper.
    - Grill the vegetables for about 3-4 minutes per side, or until they are tender and have nice grill marks. Remove from heat and let cool slightly.
2. **Prepare the Wraps:**
    - Lay out the tortillas on a flat surface.
    - Spread a generous layer of hummus on each tortilla, leaving a small border around the edges.
    - Arrange the grilled vegetables evenly over the hummus on each tortilla.
    - Top with baby spinach or mixed greens. Add crumbled feta cheese and kalamata olives if using.
3. **Wrap and Serve:**
    - Fold in the sides of each tortilla and then roll it up tightly from one end to the other.
    - Cut the wraps in half on a diagonal if desired.
    - Serve immediately or wrap tightly in foil or parchment paper for a portable option.

Enjoy your delicious and healthy Grilled Veggie and Hummus Wrap!

Gourmet Monte Cristo with Berry Jam

Ingredients:

For the Sandwich:

- 4 slices of brioche or challah bread
- 2 tablespoons Dijon mustard
- 2 tablespoons mayonnaise
- 4 slices ham
- 4 slices turkey breast
- 4 slices Swiss or Gruyère cheese
- 2 large eggs
- 1/4 cup milk
- 1/4 teaspoon ground nutmeg
- Butter or oil for frying

For the Berry Jam:

- 1/2 cup mixed berries (such as raspberries, blueberries, or strawberries)
- 1/4 cup sugar
- 1 tablespoon lemon juice

Instructions:

1. **Prepare the Berry Jam:**
   - In a small saucepan, combine mixed berries, sugar, and lemon juice.
   - Cook over medium heat, stirring frequently, until the berries break down and the mixture thickens, about 10 minutes.
   - Let cool before using.
2. **Assemble the Sandwiches:**
   - Spread Dijon mustard and mayonnaise on one side of each slice of bread.
   - Layer ham, turkey, and cheese on two of the bread slices.
   - Top with the remaining slices of bread, mustard and mayonnaise sides down, to form sandwiches.
3. **Prepare the Egg Mixture:**
   - In a bowl, whisk together eggs, milk, and ground nutmeg.
4. **Cook the Sandwiches:**
   - Heat a skillet over medium heat and add a little butter or oil.
   - Dip each sandwich into the egg mixture, ensuring it's well-coated.
   - Cook the sandwiches in the skillet until golden brown and the cheese is melted, about 3-4 minutes per side.
5. **Serve:**

- Cut the sandwiches in half and serve warm with a dollop of berry jam on the side or drizzled on top.

Enjoy your gourmet Monte Cristo with Berry Jam!

Reuben Sandwich with Homemade Sauerkraut

Ingredients:

For the Homemade Sauerkraut:

- 1 small green cabbage, finely shredded
- 1 tablespoon kosher salt
- 1 teaspoon caraway seeds (optional)
- 1 teaspoon sugar (optional)
- Water (if needed)

For the Reuben Sandwich:

- 4 slices of rye bread
- 1/2 cup Russian or Thousand Island dressing
- 8 ounces corned beef, thinly sliced
- 1 cup homemade sauerkraut (or store-bought)
- 4 slices Swiss cheese
- Butter for grilling

Instructions:

1. **Prepare the Homemade Sauerkraut:**
    - Place the shredded cabbage in a large mixing bowl.
    - Sprinkle with kosher salt, caraway seeds, and sugar (if using).
    - Massage the salt into the cabbage with your hands for about 5 minutes until the cabbage starts to release liquid.
    - Pack the cabbage mixture tightly into a clean jar or crock. Press down firmly to ensure it's submerged in its own juices. Leave some space at the top of the jar to allow for expansion.
    - Cover with a clean cloth and let it ferment at room temperature for about 3-7 days, depending on your taste preference. Check daily to ensure the cabbage is submerged. If needed, add a bit of water to keep it covered.
    - Once fermented to your liking, store the sauerkraut in the refrigerator.
2. **Assemble the Reuben Sandwiches:**
    - Spread Russian or Thousand Island dressing on one side of each slice of rye bread.
    - Layer with corned beef, sauerkraut, and Swiss cheese.
3. **Grill the Sandwiches:**
    - Heat a skillet over medium heat and add a little butter.
    - Place the assembled sandwiches in the skillet and cook until the bread is golden brown and the cheese is melted, about 3-4 minutes per side. Press down slightly with a spatula for even grilling.

4. **Serve:**
    - Remove from the skillet, cut in half if desired, and serve warm.

Enjoy your flavorful Reuben Sandwich with homemade sauerkraut!

Cuban Sandwich with Pickles and Mustard

Ingredients:

- 4 Cuban rolls or French baguettes
- 1/2 pound roast pork, sliced (or use pulled pork)
- 1/4 pound ham, sliced
- 4 slices Swiss cheese
- 1/2 cup dill pickles, sliced
- 2 tablespoons yellow mustard
- Butter for grilling

Instructions:

1. **Assemble the Sandwiches:**
   - Slice the Cuban rolls or baguettes lengthwise but not all the way through, leaving a hinge.
   - Spread yellow mustard on the inside of each roll.
   - Layer with slices of roast pork, ham, Swiss cheese, and pickles.
2. **Grill the Sandwiches:**
   - Heat a skillet or panini press over medium heat and lightly butter the outside of each sandwich.
   - Place the sandwiches in the skillet or press. Cook until the bread is crispy and golden brown, and the cheese is melted, about 3-4 minutes per side.
3. **Serve:**
   - Remove from heat, cut in half if desired, and serve warm.

Enjoy your flavorful Cuban Sandwich with Pickles and Mustard!

Fried Chicken and Pickle Sandwich

Ingredients:

For the Fried Chicken:

- 4 boneless, skinless chicken thighs
- 1 cup buttermilk
- 1 cup all-purpose flour
- 1 teaspoon paprika
- 1 teaspoon garlic powder
- 1 teaspoon onion powder
- 1/2 teaspoon cayenne pepper (optional)
- Salt and pepper to taste
- Vegetable oil for frying

For the Sandwich:

- 4 hamburger buns or sandwich rolls
- 1/2 cup mayonnaise
- 1 tablespoon pickle juice (from the pickle jar)
- 1/4 cup sliced dill pickles
- Lettuce leaves (optional)

Instructions:

1. **Marinate the Chicken:**
    - Place the chicken thighs in a bowl and cover with buttermilk. Marinate in the refrigerator for at least 1 hour or overnight.
2. **Prepare the Breading:**
    - In a separate bowl, mix together flour, paprika, garlic powder, onion powder, cayenne pepper (if using), salt, and pepper.
3. **Fry the Chicken:**
    - Heat vegetable oil in a large skillet over medium-high heat (about 350°F/175°C).
    - Dredge the marinated chicken thighs in the seasoned flour, coating them evenly.
    - Fry the chicken in batches until golden brown and cooked through, about 5-7 minutes per side. Drain on paper towels.
4. **Prepare the Sandwiches:**
    - Mix mayonnaise with pickle juice in a small bowl.
    - Spread the mayo mixture on the inside of each bun.
    - Place a fried chicken thigh on the bottom half of each bun.
    - Top with sliced dill pickles and lettuce leaves if desired.
    - Close with the top half of the bun.
5. **Serve:**

- Serve immediately while the chicken is crispy.

Enjoy your crispy Fried Chicken and Pickle Sandwich!

Mushroom and Swiss Stuffed Burger

Ingredients:

For the Stuffed Burgers:

- 1 pound ground beef (80/20 mix for juiciness)
- 1 cup mushrooms, finely chopped
- 1 tablespoon olive oil
- 1/2 cup Swiss cheese, shredded
- Salt and pepper to taste
- 1 teaspoon garlic powder (optional)
- 1 teaspoon onion powder (optional)

For Assembly:

- 4 hamburger buns
- Lettuce leaves (optional)
- Tomato slices (optional)
- Pickles (optional)
- Ketchup and mustard (optional)

Instructions:

1. **Prepare the Mushroom Filling:**
    - Heat olive oil in a skillet over medium heat.
    - Add the chopped mushrooms and cook until they release their moisture and become golden brown, about 5-7 minutes. Season with salt and pepper.
    - Let the mushrooms cool slightly, then mix in the shredded Swiss cheese.
2. **Form the Burger Patties:**
    - Divide the ground beef into 8 equal portions.
    - Flatten each portion into a thin patty.
    - Place a spoonful of the mushroom and cheese mixture in the center of 4 patties.
    - Top each with another patty and pinch the edges together to seal. Make sure the filling is completely enclosed.
3. **Cook the Burgers:**
    - Preheat a grill or skillet over medium-high heat.
    - Season the outside of the patties with salt, pepper, garlic powder, and onion powder if desired.
    - Grill or pan-fry the burgers for about 5-7 minutes per side, or until they reach your desired level of doneness. The cheese inside should be melted and gooey.
4. **Assemble the Burgers:**
    - Toast the hamburger buns if desired.
    - Place the cooked burgers on the buns.

- Add lettuce, tomato slices, pickles, and any condiments you like.
5. **Serve:**
    - Serve the burgers hot and enjoy the savory mushroom and Swiss filling!

Enjoy your delicious Mushroom and Swiss Stuffed Burger!

Braised Lamb and Mint Yogurt Flatbread

Ingredients:

For the Braised Lamb:

- 1 pound lamb shoulder or leg, cut into chunks
- 2 tablespoons olive oil
- 1 onion, chopped
- 3 cloves garlic, minced
- 1 cup beef or chicken broth
- 1/2 cup red wine (optional)
- 1 tablespoon tomato paste
- 1 teaspoon ground cumin
- 1 teaspoon ground coriander
- 1/2 teaspoon smoked paprika
- Salt and pepper to taste
- 1 bay leaf

For the Mint Yogurt Sauce:

- 1 cup plain Greek yogurt
- 1/4 cup fresh mint leaves, finely chopped
- 1 tablespoon lemon juice
- 1 garlic clove, minced
- Salt and pepper to taste

For the Flatbread:

- 4 store-bought or homemade flatbreads
- Olive oil (for brushing)

Instructions:

1. **Braised Lamb:**
    - Heat olive oil in a large pot over medium-high heat.
    - Add lamb chunks and brown on all sides. Remove and set aside.
    - In the same pot, add chopped onion and garlic; cook until softened.
    - Stir in tomato paste, cumin, coriander, smoked paprika, salt, and pepper.
    - Return the lamb to the pot, add broth, red wine (if using), and bay leaf.
    - Bring to a simmer, cover, and cook on low heat for about 2-2.5 hours, or until the lamb is tender and easily shreddable.
    - Shred the lamb with two forks and mix well with the cooking liquid. Remove the bay leaf.
2. **Mint Yogurt Sauce:**

- In a bowl, combine Greek yogurt, chopped mint, lemon juice, minced garlic, salt, and pepper.
- Mix well and adjust seasoning if needed.
3. **Prepare the Flatbread:**
    - Preheat your oven to 400°F (200°C).
    - Brush the flatbreads with olive oil.
    - Place them on a baking sheet and warm in the oven for about 5 minutes.
4. **Assemble the Flatbreads:**
    - Spread a layer of the shredded lamb mixture evenly over each warm flatbread.
    - Drizzle with the mint yogurt sauce.
5. **Serve:**
    - Cut into wedges or slices and serve immediately.

Enjoy your savory Braised Lamb and Mint Yogurt Flatbread!

Eggplant Parmesan Sandwich

Ingredients:

For the Eggplant:

- 1 large eggplant, sliced into 1/2-inch rounds
- 1 cup all-purpose flour
- 2 large eggs, beaten
- 2 cups breadcrumbs (preferably Italian)
- 1/2 cup grated Parmesan cheese
- Salt and pepper to taste
- Olive oil for frying

For the Sandwich:

- 4 ciabatta rolls or Italian hoagie rolls
- 1 cup marinara sauce
- 1 1/2 cups shredded mozzarella cheese
- Fresh basil leaves (optional)
- 1/4 cup grated Parmesan cheese (for topping, optional)

Instructions:

1. **Prepare the Eggplant:**
    - Preheat your oven to 375°F (190°C) if you plan to bake the eggplant slices afterward.
    - Season the eggplant slices with salt and let them sit for about 15 minutes to draw out excess moisture. Pat dry with paper towels.
    - Set up a breading station: Place flour in one shallow dish, beaten eggs in another, and mix breadcrumbs with 1/2 cup grated Parmesan cheese in a third.
    - Dredge each eggplant slice in flour, then dip in beaten eggs, and coat with the breadcrumb mixture.
2. **Cook the Eggplant:**
    - Heat olive oil in a large skillet over medium heat.
    - Fry the eggplant slices in batches until golden brown and crispy, about 2-3 minutes per side. Drain on paper towels. Alternatively, you can bake the breaded slices: Place them on a baking sheet and bake for 25-30 minutes, flipping halfway through.
3. **Assemble the Sandwiches:**
    - Preheat a broiler if you're melting the cheese in the oven.
    - Slice the ciabatta rolls or hoagie rolls and lightly toast them if desired.
    - Spread marinara sauce on the bottom half of each roll.
    - Layer with fried eggplant slices, then sprinkle with shredded mozzarella cheese.

        - Place the sandwiches under the broiler for 2-3 minutes, or until the cheese is melted and bubbly. Keep an eye on them to prevent burning.
 4. **Garnish and Serve:**
        - Remove from the oven and sprinkle with fresh basil leaves and additional grated Parmesan cheese if desired.
        - Top with the other half of the roll and serve warm.

Enjoy your flavorful Eggplant Parmesan Sandwich!

Salami and Provolone Ciabatta

Ingredients:

- 1 ciabatta loaf
- 1/4 cup Dijon mustard or mayonnaise (or a combination)
- 4 ounces provolone cheese, sliced
- 4 ounces salami, sliced
- 1/2 cup roasted red peppers, sliced (jarred or homemade)
- 1/4 cup sliced black olives (optional)
- Fresh arugula or spinach leaves
- Olive oil (for drizzling)
- Salt and pepper to taste

Instructions:

1. **Prepare the Ciabatta:**
   - Preheat your oven to 375°F (190°C).
   - Slice the ciabatta loaf in half lengthwise.
2. **Assemble the Sandwich:**
   - Spread Dijon mustard or mayonnaise on the cut sides of the ciabatta.
   - Layer one half with provolone cheese slices, followed by salami.
   - Add roasted red peppers and sliced black olives if using.
   - Top with fresh arugula or spinach leaves.
3. **Toast the Ciabatta:**
   - Drizzle a little olive oil over the top half of the ciabatta.
   - Place the assembled sandwich on a baking sheet and bake for about 10 minutes, or until the cheese is melted and the bread is crispy.
4. **Serve:**
   - Remove from the oven, season with salt and pepper, and cut into individual portions if desired.

Enjoy your savory Salami and Provolone Ciabatta!

Chicken and Pesto Panini

Ingredients:

- 4 ciabatta rolls or slices of rustic bread
- 1/2 cup pesto sauce (store-bought or homemade)
- 2 cups cooked chicken breast, sliced or shredded
- 4 ounces provolone or mozzarella cheese, sliced
- 1/2 cup sun-dried tomatoes, sliced (optional)
- 1/4 cup fresh basil leaves (optional)
- Olive oil or butter (for grilling)

Instructions:

1. **Assemble the Panini:**
    - Spread a generous layer of pesto sauce on one side of each slice of ciabatta or bread.
    - Layer the pesto with slices of cooked chicken, provolone or mozzarella cheese, sun-dried tomatoes, and fresh basil leaves if using.
2. **Grill the Panini:**
    - Heat a panini press or a skillet over medium heat. If using a skillet, place a heavy pan or press on top of the sandwiches.
    - Brush the outside of the bread with olive oil or butter.
    - Place the sandwiches in the panini press or skillet and grill until the bread is golden brown and the cheese is melted, about 3-4 minutes per side in a skillet, or until the press indicates it's done.
3. **Serve:**
    - Remove from the heat, cut in half if desired, and serve warm.

Enjoy your tasty Chicken and Pesto Panini!

Turkey, Cranberry, and Brie Sandwich

Ingredients:

- 4 slices of crusty bread (such as sourdough or ciabatta)
- 4 ounces Brie cheese, sliced
- 1/2 cup cranberry sauce (store-bought or homemade)
- 1 cup cooked turkey breast, sliced
- 1 tablespoon Dijon mustard (optional)
- Butter for grilling

Instructions:

1. **Assemble the Sandwiches:**
    - Spread a thin layer of Dijon mustard on one side of each slice of bread, if using.
    - On two slices of bread, layer with slices of Brie cheese.
    - Top the Brie with slices of turkey breast and a generous spoonful of cranberry sauce.
    - Close the sandwiches with the remaining slices of bread.
2. **Grill the Sandwiches:**
    - Heat a skillet over medium heat.
    - Butter the outside of each sandwich.
    - Place the sandwiches in the skillet and cook until golden brown and the cheese is melted, about 3-4 minutes per side.
3. **Serve:**
    - Remove from the skillet, cut in half if desired, and serve warm.

Enjoy your delicious Turkey, Cranberry, and Brie Sandwich!

Cheddar and Apple Butter Grilled Cheese

Ingredients:

- 4 slices of bread (such as sourdough, whole wheat, or your favorite type)
- 1/2 cup apple butter
- 8 ounces sharp cheddar cheese, sliced
- 2 tablespoons butter (for grilling)
- Optional: a sprinkle of cinnamon or a few thin apple slices for added flavor

Instructions:

1. **Prepare the Bread:**
   - Spread apple butter on one side of each slice of bread.
2. **Assemble the Sandwiches:**
   - On two slices of bread (apple butter side up), layer with slices of cheddar cheese.
   - If desired, add a sprinkle of cinnamon or a few thin apple slices on top of the cheese.
   - Place the remaining slices of bread on top, apple butter side down, to form the sandwiches.
3. **Grill the Sandwiches:**
   - Heat a skillet over medium heat.
   - Butter the outside of each sandwich.
   - Place the sandwiches in the skillet and cook until golden brown and the cheese is melted, about 3-4 minutes per side.
4. **Serve:**
   - Remove from the skillet, cut in half if desired, and serve warm.

Enjoy your sweet and savory Cheddar and Apple Butter Grilled Cheese!

Beef and Blue Cheese Stuffed Pretzel Roll

Ingredients:

For the Pretzel Rolls:

- 1 1/2 cups warm water (110°F/45°C)
- 1 packet active dry yeast (2 1/4 teaspoons)
- 1/4 cup granulated sugar
- 4 cups all-purpose flour
- 1 teaspoon salt
- 1/4 cup baking soda (for boiling)
- 1 large egg, beaten (for brushing)
- Coarse sea salt (for sprinkling)

For the Beef Filling:

- 1/2 pound ground beef
- 1/4 cup blue cheese crumbles
- 1 tablespoon olive oil
- 1/4 teaspoon garlic powder
- Salt and pepper to taste

Instructions:

1. **Prepare the Pretzel Rolls:**
    - In a bowl, dissolve sugar in warm water and sprinkle yeast on top. Let sit for 5-10 minutes until foamy.
    - In a large bowl, combine flour and salt. Add the yeast mixture and mix until a dough forms. Knead the dough on a floured surface for about 5 minutes, or until smooth.
    - Place the dough in a lightly oiled bowl, cover, and let rise in a warm place for 1 hour, or until doubled in size.
2. **Prepare the Beef Filling:**
    - In a skillet, heat olive oil over medium heat. Add ground beef, garlic powder, salt, and pepper. Cook until the beef is browned and cooked through. Stir in blue cheese crumbles and let cool.
3. **Shape the Pretzel Rolls:**
    - Preheat your oven to 425°F (220°C). Line a baking sheet with parchment paper.
    - Punch down the risen dough and divide into 8 equal pieces. Flatten each piece and place a spoonful of the beef filling in the center. Pinch the edges to seal and shape into a ball.

- In a large pot, bring water to a boil and add baking soda. Carefully drop the rolls into the boiling water for 30 seconds, then remove with a slotted spoon and place on the prepared baking sheet.
- Brush each roll with beaten egg and sprinkle with coarse sea salt.
4. **Bake the Pretzel Rolls:**
    - Bake in the preheated oven for 12-15 minutes, or until golden brown.
5. **Serve:**
    - Allow rolls to cool slightly before serving. Enjoy warm.

Enjoy your Beef and Blue Cheese Stuffed Pretzel Rolls!

Sweet and Spicy Sausage Sub

Ingredients:

For the Sausage:

- 4 sweet Italian sausage links
- 1 tablespoon olive oil
- 1/4 cup honey
- 1 tablespoon hot sauce (adjust to taste)
- 1 teaspoon smoked paprika
- Salt and pepper to taste

For the Sub:

- 4 sub rolls or hoagie rolls
- 1 red bell pepper, sliced
- 1 yellow bell pepper, sliced
- 1 onion, sliced
- 2 tablespoons olive oil
- 1/4 cup mayonnaise (optional)
- Fresh basil or parsley (optional, for garnish)

Instructions:

1. **Prepare the Sausage:**
    - Preheat your grill or skillet to medium heat.
    - Cook the sausage links, turning occasionally, until fully cooked and browned, about 10-12 minutes. Remove from heat and let rest.
2. **Make the Sweet and Spicy Glaze:**
    - In a small saucepan, combine honey, hot sauce, smoked paprika, salt, and pepper. Heat over medium heat until the mixture is well combined and slightly thickened, about 3-5 minutes.
3. **Prepare the Peppers and Onions:**
    - Heat olive oil in a skillet over medium heat.
    - Add sliced bell peppers and onions. Cook until softened and slightly caramelized, about 10 minutes.
4. **Assemble the Subs:**
    - Slice the sub rolls and lightly toast them if desired.
    - Spread mayonnaise on the inside of each roll if using.
    - Slice the cooked sausages lengthwise and place them in the rolls.
    - Top with sautéed peppers and onions.
    - Drizzle with the sweet and spicy glaze.
5. **Serve:**

- Garnish with fresh basil or parsley if desired.
  - Serve warm and enjoy!

Enjoy your Sweet and Spicy Sausage Sub!

Grilled Chicken Caesar Wrap

Ingredients:

- 2 large chicken breasts
- 1 tablespoon olive oil
- 1 tablespoon lemon juice
- 1 teaspoon garlic powder
- 1 teaspoon dried oregano
- Salt and pepper to taste
- 1 cup Caesar dressing
- 1/2 cup grated Parmesan cheese
- 2 cups Romaine lettuce, chopped
- 4 large flour tortillas or wraps

Instructions:

1. **Prepare the Chicken:**
    - Preheat your grill or skillet to medium-high heat.
    - Brush chicken breasts with olive oil, lemon juice, garlic powder, oregano, salt, and pepper.
    - Grill the chicken for 6-7 minutes per side, or until fully cooked and internal temperature reaches 165°F (74°C). Let rest before slicing.
2. **Assemble the Wraps:**
    - Slice the grilled chicken into strips.
    - In a bowl, toss chopped Romaine lettuce with Caesar dressing and grated Parmesan cheese.
    - Lay out the tortillas on a flat surface. Place a portion of the dressed lettuce in the center of each tortilla.
    - Top with sliced grilled chicken.
3. **Wrap and Serve:**
    - Fold in the sides of the tortilla and roll up tightly.
    - Slice in half if desired and serve immediately.

Enjoy your Grilled Chicken Caesar Wrap!

Pulled Pork and Pineapple Slaw Sandwich

Ingredients:

For the Pulled Pork:

- 2 pounds pork shoulder or pork butt
- 1 onion, chopped
- 3 cloves garlic, minced
- 1 cup barbecue sauce (your favorite)
- 1/2 cup chicken broth
- 1 tablespoon apple cider vinegar
- Salt and pepper to taste

For the Pineapple Slaw:

- 2 cups shredded cabbage
- 1 cup fresh pineapple, finely chopped
- 1/4 cup mayonnaise
- 1 tablespoon honey
- 1 tablespoon lime juice
- Salt and pepper to taste

For Assembly:

- 4 hamburger buns or sandwich rolls
- Pickled jalapeños (optional)

Instructions:

1. **Prepare the Pulled Pork:**
    - In a slow cooker, combine chopped onion, minced garlic, barbecue sauce, chicken broth, apple cider vinegar, salt, and pepper.
    - Add the pork shoulder and coat with the mixture.
    - Cook on low for 8 hours, or on high for 4-5 hours, until the pork is tender and easily shredded.
    - Shred the pork with two forks and mix with the sauce.
2. **Make the Pineapple Slaw:**
    - In a large bowl, combine shredded cabbage and chopped pineapple.
    - In a small bowl, mix mayonnaise, honey, lime juice, salt, and pepper.
    - Toss the cabbage mixture with the dressing until well coated.
3. **Assemble the Sandwiches:**
    - Toast the buns if desired.
    - Pile the pulled pork onto the bottom half of each bun.
    - Top with a generous amount of pineapple slaw.

        - Add pickled jalapeños if using.
4. **Serve:**
        - Close the sandwiches with the top half of the buns and serve immediately.

Enjoy your Pulled Pork and Pineapple Slaw Sandwich!

Crispy Tofu Banh Mi

Ingredients:

For the Crispy Tofu:

- 1 block firm tofu, drained and pressed
- 1/2 cup all-purpose flour
- 1/2 cup cornstarch
- 1 teaspoon garlic powder
- 1 teaspoon onion powder
- 1/2 teaspoon paprika
- Salt and pepper to taste
- 1 cup vegetable oil (for frying)

For the Pickled Vegetables:

- 1 cup shredded carrots
- 1 cup thinly sliced daikon radish
- 1/2 cup rice vinegar
- 1/4 cup sugar
- 1/4 cup water
- 1/2 teaspoon salt

For the Sandwich:

- 4 baguettes or ciabatta rolls
- 1/2 cup mayonnaise
- 1 tablespoon sriracha (optional, for a spicy kick)
- 1/2 cup cucumber, thinly sliced
- Fresh cilantro leaves
- Fresh jalapeño slices (optional)
- Sliced cucumber (optional)

Instructions:

1. **Prepare the Pickled Vegetables:**
    - In a bowl, combine rice vinegar, sugar, water, and salt. Stir until the sugar and salt are dissolved.
    - Add shredded carrots and sliced daikon radish. Mix well.
    - Cover and refrigerate for at least 30 minutes to allow the flavors to meld.
2. **Prepare the Crispy Tofu:**
    - Cut the tofu into 1/2-inch slices or cubes.
    - In a shallow dish, mix flour, cornstarch, garlic powder, onion powder, paprika, salt, and pepper.

- Dredge each tofu piece in the flour mixture, ensuring it is well-coated.
- Heat vegetable oil in a skillet over medium-high heat.
- Fry the tofu pieces in batches until golden brown and crispy, about 3-4 minutes per side. Drain on paper towels.

3. **Prepare the Sandwich:**
   - Mix mayonnaise and sriracha together if using.
   - Slice the baguettes or ciabatta rolls lengthwise.
   - Spread the spicy mayo on the inside of each roll.
   - Layer with crispy tofu, pickled vegetables, cucumber slices, cilantro leaves, and jalapeño slices if desired.
4. **Serve:**
   - Close the sandwiches, cut in half if desired, and serve immediately.

Enjoy your Crispy Tofu Banh Mi!

Tuna Melt with Capers and Pickles

Ingredients:

- 2 cans (5 ounces each) tuna, drained
- 1/4 cup mayonnaise
- 1 tablespoon Dijon mustard
- 1 tablespoon capers, chopped
- 1/4 cup pickles, finely chopped
- 1 small red onion, finely chopped (optional)
- Salt and pepper to taste
- 4 slices of bread (such as sourdough or whole grain)
- 4 ounces Swiss or cheddar cheese, sliced
- 2 tablespoons butter (for grilling)

Instructions:

1. **Prepare the Tuna Mixture:**
    - In a bowl, mix together drained tuna, mayonnaise, Dijon mustard, chopped capers, pickles, and red onion if using.
    - Season with salt and pepper to taste.
2. **Assemble the Tuna Melts:**
    - Spread the tuna mixture evenly over two slices of bread.
    - Top each with cheese slices.
    - Place the remaining slices of bread on top to form sandwiches.
3. **Grill the Sandwiches:**
    - Heat a skillet over medium heat.
    - Butter the outside of each sandwich.
    - Grill the sandwiches for about 3-4 minutes per side, or until the bread is golden brown and the cheese is melted.
4. **Serve:**
    - Remove from the skillet, cut in half if desired, and serve warm.

Enjoy your Tuna Melt with Capers and Pickles!

BBQ Chicken and Cheddar Sandwich

Ingredients:

- 2 cups cooked chicken breast, shredded or diced
- 1 cup barbecue sauce (your favorite)
- 4 slices of cheddar cheese
- 4 sandwich rolls or ciabatta buns
- 1/4 cup mayonnaise (optional)
- 1/4 cup thinly sliced red onion (optional)
- Pickle slices (optional)
- Fresh cilantro leaves (optional)

Instructions:

1. **Prepare the BBQ Chicken:**
    - In a bowl, toss the shredded or diced chicken with barbecue sauce until well-coated.
2. **Assemble the Sandwiches:**
    - If using mayonnaise, spread it on the inside of each roll or bun.
    - Divide the BBQ chicken mixture evenly among the rolls.
    - Top each with a slice of cheddar cheese.
3. **Grill or Toast the Sandwiches:**
    - Preheat a skillet over medium heat.
    - Place the sandwiches in the skillet and cook until the cheese is melted and the bread is golden brown, about 3-4 minutes per side.
4. **Serve:**
    - Add thinly sliced red onion, pickle slices, or fresh cilantro if desired.
    - Serve warm.

Enjoy your BBQ Chicken and Cheddar Sandwich!

Avocado and Tomato Basil Sandwich

Ingredients:

- 2 ripe avocados
- 1 tablespoon lemon juice
- 1/2 teaspoon garlic powder
- Salt and pepper to taste
- 4 slices of whole grain or sourdough bread
- 2 large tomatoes, sliced
- 1/4 cup fresh basil leaves
- 2 tablespoons mayonnaise (optional)
- Olive oil (optional, for drizzling)
- Red pepper flakes (optional, for a bit of heat)

Instructions:

1. **Prepare the Avocado Spread:**
    - In a bowl, mash the avocados with a fork.
    - Stir in lemon juice, garlic powder, salt, and pepper. Adjust seasoning to taste.
2. **Prepare the Bread:**
    - Toast the slices of bread if desired.
3. **Assemble the Sandwiches:**
    - Spread mayonnaise on one side of each slice of bread if using.
    - Spread the avocado mixture evenly over two of the bread slices.
    - Top the avocado with tomato slices and fresh basil leaves.
    - Drizzle with a little olive oil if desired, and sprinkle with red pepper flakes for a touch of heat.
    - Place the remaining slices of bread on top to complete the sandwiches.
4. **Serve:**
    - Cut the sandwiches in half if desired and serve immediately.

Enjoy your fresh and flavorful Avocado and Tomato Basil Sandwich!

Beef Stroganoff Sandwich with Mushrooms

Ingredients:

For the Beef Stroganoff:

- 1 pound beef sirloin or tenderloin, thinly sliced
- 2 tablespoons olive oil
- 1 small onion, finely chopped
- 2 cloves garlic, minced
- 1 cup mushrooms, sliced (cremini or button mushrooms work well)
- 1 tablespoon all-purpose flour
- 1 cup beef broth
- 1 tablespoon Worcestershire sauce
- 1 teaspoon Dijon mustard
- 1/2 cup sour cream
- Salt and pepper to taste

For the Sandwich:

- 4 slices of crusty bread (such as sourdough or ciabatta)
- 1 tablespoon butter (for toasting the bread)
- Fresh parsley, chopped (for garnish, optional)

Instructions:

1. **Prepare the Beef Stroganoff:**
    - Heat olive oil in a large skillet over medium-high heat.
    - Add the sliced beef and cook until browned on all sides. Remove the beef from the skillet and set aside.
    - In the same skillet, add the chopped onion and cook until softened, about 3-4 minutes.
    - Add the garlic and mushrooms, cooking until the mushrooms are tender.
    - Stir in the flour and cook for 1 minute to form a roux.
    - Gradually add beef broth, Worcestershire sauce, and Dijon mustard, stirring constantly until the sauce begins to thicken.
    - Return the beef to the skillet and simmer for 5 minutes.
    - Reduce heat to low and stir in the sour cream. Season with salt and pepper to taste.
2. **Prepare the Sandwiches:**
    - Butter one side of each bread slice.
    - Toast the bread in a skillet or toaster until golden brown.
3. **Assemble the Sandwiches:**

- Spoon the beef stroganoff mixture onto the non-buttered side of two slices of bread.
- Top with the remaining slices of bread, buttered side up.
4. **Serve:**
    - Serve warm, garnished with chopped fresh parsley if desired.

Enjoy your Beef Stroganoff Sandwich with Mushrooms!

Crispy Fish Sandwich with Remoulade Sauce

Ingredients:

For the Crispy Fish:

- 4 white fish fillets (such as cod, tilapia, or haddock)
- 1 cup all-purpose flour
- 1 teaspoon paprika
- 1 teaspoon garlic powder
- 1 teaspoon onion powder
- 1/2 teaspoon salt
- 1/2 teaspoon black pepper
- 2 large eggs, beaten
- 1 cup panko breadcrumbs
- Vegetable oil (for frying)

For the Remoulade Sauce:

- 1/2 cup mayonnaise
- 2 tablespoons Dijon mustard
- 1 tablespoon lemon juice
- 1 tablespoon capers, chopped
- 1 tablespoon fresh parsley, chopped
- 1 teaspoon hot sauce (adjust to taste)
- 1 clove garlic, minced
- Salt and pepper to taste

For Assembly:

- 4 hamburger buns or sandwich rolls
- Lettuce leaves
- Tomato slices
- Pickle slices

Instructions:

1. **Prepare the Remoulade Sauce:**
   - In a bowl, combine mayonnaise, Dijon mustard, lemon juice, chopped capers, parsley, hot sauce, and minced garlic.
   - Mix well and season with salt and pepper to taste.
   - Refrigerate until ready to use.
2. **Prepare the Crispy Fish:**
   - In a shallow dish, mix flour, paprika, garlic powder, onion powder, salt, and pepper.

    - In another shallow dish, place the beaten eggs.
    - In a third shallow dish, place panko breadcrumbs.
    - Dredge each fish fillet in the seasoned flour, shaking off excess.
    - Dip in the beaten eggs, then coat with panko breadcrumbs.
    - Heat vegetable oil in a skillet over medium-high heat.
    - Fry the fish fillets until golden brown and crispy, about 3-4 minutes per side. Drain on paper towels.
3. **Assemble the Sandwiches:**
    - Toast the buns if desired.
    - Spread a generous amount of remoulade sauce on the bottom half of each bun.
    - Top with a crispy fish fillet.
    - Add lettuce leaves, tomato slices, and pickle slices.
    - Spread additional remoulade sauce on the top half of the bun if desired, then close the sandwich.
4. **Serve:**
    - Serve immediately and enjoy your Crispy Fish Sandwich with Remoulade Sauce!

This sandwich is perfect for a satisfying and flavorful meal. Enjoy!

Turkey Club with Avocado and Bacon

Ingredients:

- 8 slices of bread (such as whole grain, sourdough, or ciabatta)
- 4 ounces turkey breast, sliced (deli-style or cooked)
- 4 slices of bacon
- 1 avocado, sliced
- 2 tomatoes, sliced
- Lettuce leaves (such as Romaine or iceberg)
- 1/4 cup mayonnaise
- 1 tablespoon Dijon mustard
- Salt and pepper to taste

Instructions:

1. **Cook the Bacon:**
   - In a skillet over medium heat, cook the bacon until crispy, about 4-5 minutes per side. Remove from the skillet and drain on paper towels.
2. **Prepare the Spread:**
   - In a small bowl, mix together the mayonnaise and Dijon mustard. Season with salt and pepper to taste.
3. **Toast the Bread:**
   - Toast the slices of bread until golden brown.
4. **Assemble the Sandwiches:**
   - Spread the mayo-mustard mixture on one side of each slice of toasted bread.
   - On four of the bread slices, layer turkey slices, crispy bacon, avocado slices, tomato slices, and lettuce leaves.
   - Top with the remaining slices of bread, mayo-mustard side down.
5. **Serve:**
   - Cut the sandwiches in half diagonally if desired.
   - Serve immediately and enjoy!

This Turkey Club with Avocado and Bacon is a classic and satisfying sandwich with a delicious mix of flavors and textures. Enjoy!

Braised Beef Brisket with Horseradish Cream

Ingredients:

For the Braised Brisket:

- 3 to 4 pounds beef brisket
- 2 tablespoons olive oil
- 1 onion, chopped
- 3 cloves garlic, minced
- 2 cups beef broth
- 1 cup red wine (optional, or more beef broth)
- 2 tablespoons tomato paste
- 2 carrots, sliced
- 2 celery stalks, sliced
- 2 sprigs fresh thyme
- 2 bay leaves
- Salt and pepper to taste

For the Horseradish Cream:

- 1/2 cup sour cream
- 2 tablespoons prepared horseradish (adjust to taste)
- 1 tablespoon Dijon mustard
- 1 tablespoon lemon juice
- Salt and pepper to taste

Instructions:

1. **Prepare the Brisket:**
   - Preheat your oven to 325°F (165°C).
   - Season the brisket generously with salt and pepper.
   - Heat olive oil in a large ovenproof pot or Dutch oven over medium-high heat.
   - Sear the brisket on all sides until browned, about 4-5 minutes per side. Remove from the pot and set aside.
2. **Cook the Vegetables:**
   - In the same pot, add chopped onion, garlic, carrots, and celery. Cook until softened, about 5-7 minutes.
   - Stir in tomato paste and cook for 1 minute.
3. **Braised Brisket:**
   - Return the brisket to the pot.
   - Add beef broth, red wine (if using), thyme, and bay leaves.
   - Bring to a simmer, then cover and transfer to the oven.

- Braise for 3 to 4 hours, or until the brisket is tender and easily shredded with a fork.
4. **Prepare the Horseradish Cream:**
    - In a small bowl, mix together sour cream, prepared horseradish, Dijon mustard, and lemon juice.
    - Season with salt and pepper to taste. Refrigerate until ready to use.
5. **Serve:**
    - Remove the brisket from the pot and let it rest for 10-15 minutes before slicing.
    - Serve the sliced brisket with the braising liquid spooned over the top and a dollop of horseradish cream on the side.

Enjoy your Braised Beef Brisket with Horseradish Cream!

Buffalo Cauliflower Wrap

Ingredients:

For the Buffalo Cauliflower:

- 1 head cauliflower, cut into florets
- 1 cup all-purpose flour
- 1 cup water (or buttermilk for extra richness)
- 1 teaspoon garlic powder
- 1 teaspoon onion powder
- 1/2 teaspoon paprika
- Salt and pepper to taste
- 1 cup buffalo sauce (store-bought or homemade)

For the Wrap:

- 4 large flour tortillas or wraps
- 1/2 cup shredded lettuce
- 1/2 cup shredded carrots
- 1/2 cup sliced celery
- 1/4 cup crumbled blue cheese or feta (optional)
- Ranch or blue cheese dressing (optional)

Instructions:

1. **Prepare the Cauliflower:**
    - Preheat your oven to 450°F (230°C). Line a baking sheet with parchment paper.
    - In a large bowl, whisk together flour, water (or buttermilk), garlic powder, onion powder, paprika, salt, and pepper to make a batter.
    - Dip each cauliflower floret into the batter, coating evenly, and place on the baking sheet.
    - Bake for 20-25 minutes, or until the cauliflower is crispy and golden brown.
2. **Add Buffalo Sauce:**
    - Remove the cauliflower from the oven and toss in buffalo sauce until well coated. Return to the oven for an additional 5 minutes if desired for extra crispiness.
3. **Assemble the Wraps:**
    - Warm the tortillas in a dry skillet or microwave.
    - Place a tortilla on a flat surface and layer with shredded lettuce, shredded carrots, sliced celery, and buffalo cauliflower.
    - Top with crumbled blue cheese or feta, and drizzle with ranch or blue cheese dressing if using.
4. **Wrap and Serve:**
    - Fold in the sides of the tortilla and roll up tightly.

- Cut in half if desired and serve immediately.

Enjoy your flavorful and spicy Buffalo Cauliflower Wrap!

Spicy Italian Sub with Giardiniera

Ingredients:

For the Sub:

- 4 Italian sub rolls or hoagie rolls
- 1/4 pound sliced salami
- 1/4 pound sliced pepperoni
- 1/4 pound sliced ham
- 4 ounces provolone cheese, sliced
- 1/4 cup sliced red onion
- 1/4 cup sliced banana peppers (or pickled peppers)
- 1/4 cup sliced black olives

For the Giardiniera:

- 1 cup mixed vegetables (e.g., carrots, cauliflower, bell peppers), chopped
- 1/2 cup sliced jalapeños (or other hot peppers)
- 1/2 cup white vinegar
- 1/2 cup olive oil
- 2 cloves garlic, minced
- 1 teaspoon dried oregano
- 1 teaspoon dried basil
- 1 teaspoon crushed red pepper flakes (adjust to taste)
- Salt and pepper to taste

Instructions:

1. **Prepare the Giardiniera:**
    - In a bowl, combine the chopped mixed vegetables and jalapeños.
    - In a saucepan, heat olive oil, white vinegar, minced garlic, oregano, basil, crushed red pepper flakes, salt, and pepper over medium heat. Bring to a simmer for about 5 minutes to meld the flavors.
    - Pour the hot mixture over the chopped vegetables and peppers.
    - Allow to cool to room temperature, then cover and refrigerate for at least 1 hour to let the flavors develop. This can be made ahead and stored in the fridge for up to 2 weeks.
2. **Assemble the Sub:**
    - Preheat your oven to 350°F (175°C).
    - Slice the sub rolls lengthwise, but not all the way through, so they open like a book.
    - Layer the salami, pepperoni, ham, and provolone cheese on each roll.

- Place the assembled subs on a baking sheet and bake for about 5-7 minutes, or until the cheese is melted and the bread is slightly crispy.
3. **Add Toppings:**
    - Remove the subs from the oven.
    - Top each sandwich with sliced red onion, banana peppers, black olives, and a generous amount of giardiniera.
4. **Serve:**
    - Close the subs, cut in half if desired, and serve immediately.

Enjoy your Spicy Italian Sub with Giardiniera!

Grilled Chicken and Mango Chutney Sandwich

Ingredients:

For the Grilled Chicken:

- 2 boneless, skinless chicken breasts
- 2 tablespoons olive oil
- 1 teaspoon ground cumin
- 1 teaspoon paprika
- 1 teaspoon garlic powder
- 1/2 teaspoon onion powder
- 1/2 teaspoon dried thyme
- Salt and pepper to taste

For the Mango Chutney:

- 1 cup mango chutney (store-bought or homemade)
- 1 tablespoon lime juice
- 1/4 teaspoon ground ginger (optional)

For the Sandwich:

- 4 slices of bread (such as ciabatta, sourdough, or whole grain)
- 4 tablespoons mayonnaise
- 4 leaves of lettuce (such as Romaine or Butter lettuce)
- 1 ripe avocado, sliced
- Tomato slices (optional)
- Pickled red onions (optional)

Instructions:

1. **Prepare the Grilled Chicken:**
    - Preheat your grill or a grill pan to medium-high heat.
    - In a small bowl, mix olive oil, cumin, paprika, garlic powder, onion powder, dried thyme, salt, and pepper.
    - Rub the spice mixture evenly over the chicken breasts.
    - Grill the chicken for 6-7 minutes per side, or until fully cooked and the internal temperature reaches 165°F (74°C). Let rest for a few minutes before slicing.
2. **Prepare the Mango Chutney:**
    - In a small bowl, mix the mango chutney with lime juice and ground ginger (if using). Adjust the flavor to taste.
3. **Assemble the Sandwiches:**
    - Toast the bread slices if desired.
    - Spread mayonnaise on one side of each slice of bread.

- Place a leaf of lettuce on two of the bread slices.
            - Layer sliced grilled chicken on top of the lettuce.
            - Spoon a generous amount of mango chutney over the chicken.
            - Add avocado slices, tomato slices, and pickled red onions if using.
            - Top with the remaining slices of bread.
    4. **Serve:**
            - Cut the sandwiches in half if desired and serve immediately.

Enjoy your Grilled Chicken and Mango Chutney Sandwich!

Cheesy Ham and Swiss Croissant

Ingredients:

- 4 large croissants
- 4 ounces Swiss cheese, sliced
- 4 ounces cooked ham, sliced
- 2 tablespoons Dijon mustard
- 2 tablespoons butter, melted
- 1 tablespoon fresh chives, chopped (optional)
- 1 tablespoon honey (optional, for a touch of sweetness)

Instructions:

1. **Preheat Oven:**
   - Preheat your oven to 375°F (190°C).
2. **Prepare the Croissants:**
   - Slice each croissant in half horizontally, but not all the way through, so they open like a book.
3. **Assemble the Sandwiches:**
   - Spread Dijon mustard on the inside of each croissant.
   - Layer Swiss cheese and ham slices inside each croissant.
4. **Bake the Croissants:**
   - Brush the outside of the croissants with melted butter.
   - Place the croissants on a baking sheet and bake for 8-10 minutes, or until the cheese is melted and the croissants are golden brown.
5. **Finish and Serve:**
   - If desired, drizzle with honey and sprinkle with fresh chives before serving.

Enjoy your Cheesy Ham and Swiss Croissant!

Pulled Pork and Chipotle BBQ Sandwich

Ingredients:

For the Pulled Pork:

- 3-4 pounds pork shoulder (also called pork butt)
- 1 tablespoon paprika
- 1 tablespoon brown sugar
- 1 tablespoon chili powder
- 1 teaspoon garlic powder
- 1 teaspoon onion powder
- 1 teaspoon ground cumin
- 1/2 teaspoon salt
- 1/2 teaspoon black pepper
- 1 cup chicken or beef broth
- 1 large onion, sliced
- 2 cloves garlic, minced

For the Chipotle BBQ Sauce:

- 1 cup barbecue sauce (your favorite)
- 1-2 tablespoons chipotle peppers in adobo sauce, chopped (adjust to taste)
- 1 tablespoon honey
- 1 tablespoon apple cider vinegar

For the Sandwiches:

- 4 hamburger buns or sandwich rolls
- Coleslaw (optional, for topping)

Instructions:

1. **Prepare the Pulled Pork:**
    - In a small bowl, mix paprika, brown sugar, chili powder, garlic powder, onion powder, cumin, salt, and pepper.
    - Rub the spice mixture evenly over the pork shoulder.
    - Place the sliced onion and minced garlic in the bottom of a slow cooker.
    - Place the pork shoulder on top, and pour the broth around it.
    - Cook on low for 8-10 hours or on high for 4-6 hours, until the pork is tender and shreds easily.
2. **Prepare the Chipotle BBQ Sauce:**
    - In a bowl, mix barbecue sauce, chopped chipotle peppers, honey, and apple cider vinegar.
    - Adjust seasoning or spiciness to taste.

3. **Shred the Pork:**
    - Remove the pork shoulder from the slow cooker and shred with two forks.
    - Return the shredded pork to the slow cooker and mix with the cooking juices.
4. **Assemble the Sandwiches:**
    - Toast the buns if desired.
    - Pile the pulled pork onto the bottom half of each bun.
    - Spoon the chipotle BBQ sauce over the pork.
    - Top with coleslaw if desired and place the top half of the bun on each sandwich.
5. **Serve:**
    - Serve the sandwiches warm and enjoy!

This Pulled Pork and Chipotle BBQ Sandwich is sure to be a hit with its smoky, spicy flavor. Enjoy!

Pastrami on Rye with Mustard

Ingredients:

- 4 slices rye bread
- 1/2 pound pastrami, thinly sliced
- 2 tablespoons yellow mustard (or to taste)
- Pickles (optional, for serving)

Instructions:

1. **Prepare the Bread:**
    - Lightly toast the rye bread if desired.
2. **Assemble the Sandwich:**
    - Spread mustard on one side of each slice of rye bread.
    - Layer the pastrami evenly on two of the bread slices.
3. **Top and Serve:**
    - Close the sandwiches with the remaining slices of bread.
    - Serve with pickles on the side if desired.

Enjoy your simple and satisfying Pastrami on Rye with Mustard!

Classic Lobster Grilled Cheese

Ingredients:

- 1 cup cooked lobster meat, chopped
- 4 slices sourdough or brioche bread
- 4 ounces cheddar cheese, sliced (or a blend of cheddar and Gruyère)
- 2 tablespoons butter, softened
- 1 tablespoon mayonnaise
- 1 tablespoon lemon juice
- 1 tablespoon fresh chives, chopped (optional)
- Salt and pepper to taste

Instructions:

1. **Prepare the Lobster Mixture:**
    - In a bowl, mix the chopped lobster meat with mayonnaise, lemon juice, chives (if using), salt, and pepper.
2. **Assemble the Sandwiches:**
    - Spread butter on one side of each slice of bread.
    - On the non-buttered side of two slices, layer cheese slices, then spread a generous amount of the lobster mixture.
    - Top with additional cheese slices and the remaining bread slices, buttered side up.
3. **Cook the Sandwiches:**
    - Heat a skillet over medium heat.
    - Cook the sandwiches for 3-4 minutes per side, or until the bread is golden brown and the cheese is melted.
4. **Serve:**
    - Slice in half and serve warm.

Enjoy your indulgent Classic Lobster Grilled Cheese!

Spicy Tuna and Avocado Sandwich

Ingredients:

- 1 can (5 oz) tuna in oil, drained
- 1 tablespoon mayonnaise
- 1 tablespoon sriracha sauce (adjust to taste)
- 1 tablespoon lime juice
- 1 avocado, sliced
- 2 tablespoons fresh cilantro, chopped (optional)
- Salt and pepper to taste
- 4 slices of bread (such as whole grain or sourdough)
- Lettuce leaves
- Tomato slices (optional)

Instructions:

1. **Prepare the Tuna Mixture:**
    - In a bowl, combine the tuna, mayonnaise, sriracha sauce, lime juice, salt, and pepper. Mix well.
2. **Assemble the Sandwiches:**
    - Toast the bread slices if desired.
    - Spread the spicy tuna mixture evenly on two slices of bread.
    - Top with avocado slices and fresh cilantro if using.
    - Add lettuce leaves and tomato slices if desired.
    - Place the remaining bread slices on top to complete the sandwiches.
3. **Serve:**
    - Cut the sandwiches in half if desired and serve immediately.

Enjoy your flavorful Spicy Tuna and Avocado Sandwich!

Balsamic Glazed Chicken Sandwich

Ingredients:

- 2 boneless, skinless chicken breasts
- 1/2 cup balsamic glaze (store-bought or homemade)
- 2 tablespoons olive oil
- 1 teaspoon garlic powder
- 1 teaspoon dried thyme
- Salt and pepper to taste
- 4 slices of bread (such as ciabatta or baguette)
- 4 ounces fresh mozzarella cheese, sliced
- 1 cup baby spinach or arugula
- 1 tomato, sliced
- 1/4 cup mayonnaise
- 1 tablespoon Dijon mustard

Instructions:

1. **Prepare the Chicken:**
    - Preheat your grill or skillet to medium-high heat.
    - Season the chicken breasts with garlic powder, dried thyme, salt, and pepper.
    - Heat olive oil in the grill or skillet.
    - Cook the chicken breasts for 5-7 minutes per side, or until fully cooked and the internal temperature reaches 165°F (74°C).
    - Brush the chicken with balsamic glaze during the last few minutes of cooking.
2. **Prepare the Spread:**
    - In a small bowl, mix mayonnaise and Dijon mustard.
3. **Assemble the Sandwiches:**
    - Toast the bread slices if desired.
    - Spread the mayonnaise mixture on one side of each slice of bread.
    - Layer with fresh mozzarella, cooked chicken, baby spinach or arugula, and tomato slices.
    - Drizzle with extra balsamic glaze if desired.
4. **Serve:**
    - Close the sandwiches and cut in half if desired. Serve immediately.

Enjoy your Balsamic Glazed Chicken Sandwich!

Brisket and Pickled Onion Sandwich

Ingredients:

For the Brisket:

- 1 pound cooked brisket, sliced thinly (leftover or pre-cooked)
- 1/2 cup barbecue sauce (your choice)

For the Pickled Onions:

- 1 red onion, thinly sliced
- 1/2 cup white vinegar
- 1/2 cup water
- 2 tablespoons sugar
- 1 teaspoon salt
- 1/2 teaspoon mustard seeds (optional)
- 1/2 teaspoon peppercorns (optional)

For the Sandwich:

- 4 rolls or sandwich buns (such as ciabatta or hoagie rolls)
- 4 tablespoons mayonnaise (optional)
- 4-6 slices of pickles (optional)

Instructions:

1. **Prepare the Pickled Onions:**
   - In a small saucepan, combine vinegar, water, sugar, salt, mustard seeds, and peppercorns. Bring to a simmer over medium heat, stirring until the sugar and salt are dissolved.
   - Place the onion slices in a jar or bowl. Pour the hot vinegar mixture over the onions. Let cool to room temperature, then refrigerate for at least 30 minutes.
2. **Prepare the Brisket:**
   - Heat the sliced brisket in a skillet or microwave with the barbecue sauce until warmed through.
3. **Assemble the Sandwiches:**
   - Toast the rolls if desired.
   - Spread mayonnaise on the inside of the rolls if using.
   - Layer the warmed brisket on the bottom half of each roll.
   - Top with pickled onions and pickles if using.
   - Close the sandwiches with the top half of the rolls.
4. **Serve:**
   - Cut in half if desired and serve immediately.

Enjoy your Brisket and Pickled Onion Sandwich!

Stuffed Portobello Mushroom Burger

Ingredients:

For the Stuffed Mushrooms:

- 4 large Portobello mushrooms, stems removed and gills scraped out
- 4 ounces cream cheese, softened
- 1/2 cup shredded mozzarella cheese
- 1/4 cup grated Parmesan cheese
- 2 cloves garlic, minced
- 2 tablespoons fresh basil or parsley, chopped
- 1/2 teaspoon dried oregano
- Salt and pepper to taste

For the Burger Assembly:

- 4 burger buns
- Lettuce leaves
- Tomato slices
- Red onion slices
- Pickles (optional)
- Olive oil for brushing

Instructions:

1. **Prepare the Stuffed Mushrooms:**
    - Preheat your oven to 375°F (190°C).
    - In a bowl, mix the cream cheese, mozzarella cheese, Parmesan cheese, minced garlic, chopped basil or parsley, dried oregano, salt, and pepper until well combined.
    - Brush the Portobello mushrooms with olive oil and season with a little salt and pepper.
    - Spoon the cheese mixture into each mushroom cap, packing it in slightly.
2. **Bake the Mushrooms:**
    - Place the stuffed mushrooms on a baking sheet.
    - Bake in the preheated oven for about 20 minutes, or until the mushrooms are tender and the cheese is melted and slightly golden.
3. **Prepare the Burger Buns:**
    - While the mushrooms are baking, toast the burger buns in a skillet or under the broiler until golden brown.
4. **Assemble the Burgers:**
    - Place a stuffed Portobello mushroom on the bottom half of each bun.
    - Top with lettuce, tomato slices, red onion slices, and pickles if desired.

        - Close with the top half of the bun.
5. **Serve:**
        - Serve immediately and enjoy your delicious Stuffed Portobello Mushroom Burger!

This burger is a hearty, satisfying vegetarian option that's packed with flavor. Enjoy!

Pork Schnitzel Sandwich with Cabbage Slaw

Ingredients:

For the Pork Schnitzel:

- 4 boneless pork chops or cutlets, pounded thin
- 1 cup all-purpose flour
- 2 large eggs, beaten
- 1 1/2 cups panko breadcrumbs
- 1/2 cup grated Parmesan cheese
- 1 teaspoon paprika
- Salt and pepper to taste
- Vegetable oil for frying

For the Cabbage Slaw:

- 2 cups shredded cabbage (green or red)
- 1 carrot, grated
- 1/4 cup mayonnaise
- 1 tablespoon apple cider vinegar
- 1 tablespoon sugar
- Salt and pepper to taste

For the Sandwich:

- 4 sandwich rolls or brioche buns
- 1 tablespoon Dijon mustard (optional)
- Pickles (optional)

Instructions:

1. **Prepare the Pork Schnitzel:**
   - Set up a breading station: Place flour in one bowl, beaten eggs in another, and panko breadcrumbs mixed with Parmesan, paprika, salt, and pepper in a third bowl.
   - Dredge each pork cutlet in flour, then dip in beaten eggs, and coat with the breadcrumb mixture.
   - Heat vegetable oil in a skillet over medium-high heat.
   - Fry the pork cutlets for 3-4 minutes per side, or until golden brown and cooked through. Drain on paper towels.
2. **Prepare the Cabbage Slaw:**
   - In a large bowl, combine shredded cabbage and grated carrot.
   - In a small bowl, whisk together mayonnaise, apple cider vinegar, sugar, salt, and pepper.

- Toss the cabbage mixture with the dressing until well coated. Refrigerate until ready to use.
3. **Assemble the Sandwiches:**
    - Toast the rolls or buns if desired.
    - Spread Dijon mustard on the bottom half of each roll if using.
    - Place a pork schnitzel on each roll.
    - Top with a generous amount of cabbage slaw.
    - Add pickles if desired and close with the top half of the roll.
4. **Serve:**
    - Serve immediately and enjoy!

This Pork Schnitzel Sandwich with Cabbage Slaw combines crispy, flavorful schnitzel with tangy, crunchy slaw for a delicious meal.

Crispy Chicken Sandwich with Garlic Aioli

Ingredients:

For the Crispy Chicken:

- 4 boneless, skinless chicken thighs (or breasts)
- 1 cup buttermilk
- 1 cup all-purpose flour
- 1 cup panko breadcrumbs
- 1 teaspoon paprika
- 1 teaspoon garlic powder
- 1 teaspoon onion powder
- 1/2 teaspoon cayenne pepper (optional)
- Salt and pepper to taste
- Vegetable oil for frying

For the Garlic Aioli:

- 1/2 cup mayonnaise
- 2 cloves garlic, minced
- 1 tablespoon lemon juice
- 1 tablespoon olive oil
- Salt and pepper to taste

For the Sandwich:

- 4 sandwich buns
- Lettuce leaves
- Tomato slices
- Pickles (optional)

Instructions:

1. **Prepare the Crispy Chicken:**
    - Marinate the chicken in buttermilk for at least 1 hour or overnight in the refrigerator.
    - In a shallow dish, mix flour, paprika, garlic powder, onion powder, cayenne pepper (if using), salt, and pepper.
    - In another dish, place the panko breadcrumbs.
    - Dredge each chicken piece in the flour mixture, then dip in buttermilk again, and coat with panko breadcrumbs.
    - Heat vegetable oil in a skillet over medium-high heat.
    - Fry the chicken for 5-6 minutes per side, or until golden brown and cooked through. Drain on paper towels.

2. **Prepare the Garlic Aioli:**
   - In a bowl, mix mayonnaise, minced garlic, lemon juice, olive oil, salt, and pepper until smooth. Adjust seasoning to taste.
3. **Assemble the Sandwiches:**
   - Toast the sandwich buns if desired.
   - Spread garlic aioli on the bottom half of each bun.
   - Place a crispy chicken piece on each bun.
   - Top with lettuce, tomato slices, and pickles if using.
   - Close with the top half of the bun.
4. **Serve:**
   - Serve immediately and enjoy!

This Crispy Chicken Sandwich with Garlic Aioli is a flavorful, crispy treat that's perfect for a satisfying meal.

Hot Turkey Sandwich with Gravy

Ingredients:

For the Turkey Sandwich:

- 4 slices of bread (such as white or whole wheat)
- 2 cups cooked turkey breast, sliced or shredded
- 4 tablespoons butter (for toasting the bread)
- 1 cup turkey or chicken gravy (store-bought or homemade)

For Homemade Gravy (if needed):

- 2 tablespoons butter
- 2 tablespoons all-purpose flour
- 1 cup turkey or chicken broth
- Salt and pepper to taste

Instructions:

1. **Prepare the Gravy:**
    - In a saucepan, melt butter over medium heat.
    - Add flour and cook, stirring constantly, for about 1-2 minutes to form a roux.
    - Gradually whisk in the broth, ensuring there are no lumps.
    - Simmer for 3-5 minutes, or until the gravy thickens. Season with salt and pepper to taste.
2. **Prepare the Turkey:**
    - Heat the sliced or shredded turkey in a skillet over medium heat, adding a bit of gravy to keep it moist.
3. **Assemble the Sandwiches:**
    - Butter one side of each bread slice.
    - Toast the bread slices in a skillet over medium heat until golden brown and crispy.
    - Place a slice of toasted bread on each plate.
    - Pile the warm turkey on top of the bread.
    - Spoon additional gravy over the turkey.
4. **Serve:**
    - Top with another slice of toasted bread if desired, or serve open-faced.
    - Serve immediately with extra gravy on the side if desired.

Enjoy your hearty Hot Turkey Sandwich with Gravy!

www.ingramcontent.com/pod-product-compliance
Lightning Source LLC
LaVergne TN
LVHW081615060526
838201LV00054B/2266